Art and Theosophy

Also in this series:

Theosophy and the Search for Happiness
Texts by Moon Laramie and Annie Besant

Theosophy and Esoteric Christianity
*Texts by Isis Resende, R. Heber Newton
& Franz Hartmann*

Forthcoming:

Theosophy and Clairvoyance
Texts by Kurt Leland and C.W. Leadbeater

Theosophy and Social Justice
*Texts by Dr. Barbara B. Hebert, William Quan Judge
& Annie Besant*

Theosophy and Yoga
Texts by Jenny Baker and Annie Besant

Art & Theosophy

TEXTS BY MARTIN FIRRELL
AND A. L. POGOSKY

martin firrell company
MODERN THEOSOPHY

First published in 2019 by Martin Firrell Company Ltd.
10 Queen Street Place, London EC4R 1AG, United Kingdom.

ISBN 978-1-912622-08-5

Design © Copyright Martin Firrell Company 2019.
Introduction © Copyright Moon Laramie 2019.
Essay © Copyright Martin Firrell 2019.

All rights reserved. No part of this publication may be reproduced, stored in or introduced into a retrieval system, or transmitted, in any form, or by any means (electronic, mechanical, photocopying, recording or otherwise) without the prior written consent of the publisher.

This book is sold subject to the condition that it shall not, by way of trade or otherwise, be lent, re-sold, hired out, or otherwise circulated without the publisher's prior consent in any form of binding or cover other than that in which it is published and without a similar condition including this condition being imposed on the subsequent purchaser.

Text is set in Baskerville, 12pt on 18pt.

Baskerville is a serif typeface designed in 1754 by John Baskerville (1706–1775) in Birmingham, England. Compared to earlier typeface designs, Baskerville increased the contrast between thick and thin strokes. Serifs were made sharper and more tapered, and the axis of rounded letters was placed in a more vertical position. The curved strokes were made more circular in shape, and the characters became more regular.

Baskerville is categorised as a transitional typeface between classical typefaces and high contrast modern faces. Of his own typeface, John Baskerville wrote, 'Having been an early admirer of the beauty of letters, I became insensibly desirous of contributing to the perfection of them. I formed to myself ideas of greater accuracy than had yet appeared, and had endeavoured to produce a set of types according to what I conceived to be their true proportion.'

Introduction
by Moon Laramie

ART AND THEOSOPHY

This volume of the *Modern Theosophy* series features writing by the public artist Martin Firrell and the art promoter and activist A.L. Pogosky. Among the themes explored are the relationship between consciousness and art, the creative process as an act of love and the place of art in the theosophical tradition. As people committed to the arts, both Firrell and Pogosky's contributions touch on the ideas of brotherhood and cooperation, one of the three core principles in theosophy.

One thing which sets humanity apart from the animal kingdom is our ability to express ourselves through art, literature and music. Human beings are self-aware and with that self-awareness comes an appreciation of the beauty in the natural world. A.L. Pogosky observes how human beings seem happier when closer to nature. According to Pogosky, art awakens the innermost soul of the individual, so that he or she 'grows from within, as the flower grows'.

Both Firrell and Pogosky are concerned with the way we see ourselves reflected in the arts and our relationship to them. The theosophical author C. Jinarajadasa observes that true art 'will always call forth a response in man from the higher intuition, the Buddhi… Art, then, is a means for the quickening of the Buddhi whence come swift generalisations from within of the meaning of life's activities, and the hastening of evolution'.[1] Martin Firrell's comments about his personal experience of making art echo this sentiment: 'My own subjective experience of practising as an artist suggests that ideas sometimes appear spontaneously and fully formed. It is as if they have been transmitted rather than created. They do indeed seem to 'flow through' from some other realm…'

According to theosophy, evolution is the unfolding of a divine plan. Everything that takes place in the cosmos is directed by a superlunary intelligence. This idea has also been explored in science. The physicists John D. Barrow, Frank J. Tipler and John Archibald Wheeler have proposed theories supporting panpsychism and a consciously determined universe. According to Wheeler, 'We are participators in bringing into being not only the near and here but the far away and long ago. We are in this sense, participators in bringing about something of the universe…'[2] This mirrors the words of Hilma af Klint for whom artistic expression was a process of connection with the divine: 'The pictures were painted directly through me, without any preliminary drawings, and with great force.' Art can be seen as an expression of divine wisdom. In this volume, A.L. Pogosky refers to artistic expression as 'the most sacred outlet for the Soul to reach God'. Many theosophical writers agree. Gottfried De Purucker suggests that art provides 'the foundation of our own civilization and thinking, and the as yet unrecognised inspiration by heritage and transmission of the best that we have'.[3]

C. Jinarajadasa describes true genius as 'the ability of the human soul to come into touch with the World of Ideas'.[4] *Art and Theosophy* alludes to the way art allows us to view the world from multiple angles, seeing it for how it truly is rather than how we might have been conditioned to see it. In many ways art serves as a barometer of humanity's progress on the evolutionary journey towards revelation.

'For Art is life at its intensest, and reveals the beauty and worth of all human activities; and yet it shall be the mission of Art, now and for ever, to show men that Life, even in all its fullness, is like "a dome of many-colored glass", reflecting but broken gleams of "the white radiance of Eternity".'[5]

1. C. Jinarajadasa, *Art as a Factor in the Soul's Evolution*, Theosophical Publishing House, 1915.

2. *The Science Show: The Anthropic Universe*, NBC Radio, 2006.

3. Gottfried de Purucker, *The Esoteric Tradition*, Theosophical University Press, 1935.

4. C. Jinarajadasa, *Art as a Factor in the Soul's Evolution*, Theosophical Publishing House, 1915.

5. Ibid.

Martin Firrell

Martin Firrell, born 1963, is a French public artist, stimulating debate in public space to promote positive social change. He uses language to engage directly with the public, promoting constructive dialogues, usually about marginalisation, equality and more equitable social organisation, with the aim of making the world more humane. His work has been summarised as 'art as debate'.

It was a passage in Anaïs Nin's novel *The Four Chambered Heart* that set Firrell on the path of socially engaged public works. In the passage in question, the novel's protagonist declares that literature fails to prepare us for, or guide us through, the calamities or challenges of life, and is therefore worthless. Firrell sets out to remedy Nin's 'worthlessness' of words by using simple and direct language to raise provocative questions about society, relevant to the vast majority of people and freely available in public.

Firrell trained originally as an advertising copywriter and British social historian Joe Moran suggests Firrell is consequently well equipped to hijack public space with stealthily subversive declarations like 'Protest is liberty's ally'.

Firrell has used digital billboards, cinema screens, newsprint, the internet, portraiture and video interviews of culturally significant figures like the Booker Prize winning novelist Howard Jacobson, Britain's first transgender woman April Ashley, Johnson Beharry VC, and the philosopher A. C. Grayling. He has used large-scale digital projection onto the Guards' Chapel, spiritual home of the Household Division of the British Army, the National Gallery in London, the Houses of Parliament, the Royal Opera House, Tate Britain, and St Paul's Cathedral.

Firrell has worked with complex and influential organisations, including the Church of England (St Paul's Cathedral, 2008) and the British Army (Household Division, 2009).

Canon Martin Warner, commissioner of Firrell's work for St Paul's, commented in the cathedral's 2008 Annual Report that Firrell possesses 'a genius for creating partnerships'. Arguably, it is this ability that has enabled organisations to engage confidently with audacious, self-questioning project content, including 'I don't think this is what God intended' (West Front, St

Paul's Cathedral) and 'War is always a failure' (North elevation, Guards' Chapel).

In 2006, Martin Firrell was described in the Guardian newspaper as 'one of the capital's most influential public artists'.

Art and Theosophy
by Martin Firrell (2019)

Where Does Art Come From?

When the Swedish painter Hilma af Klint (1862-1944) painted images for what she termed the 'Temple', she became the world's first abstract artist. Wassily Kandinsky (1866-1944) has long been credited with being the first purely abstract painter but a considerable body of af Klint's work predates Kandinsky's. It seems important to put the record straight - a woman and a theosophist was the original pioneer of abstraction. Hilma was one of a group of five women called 'De Fem' or 'The Five' who believed it was possible to make contact with 'High Masters' or beings on another, higher spiritual plane. Hilma af Klint painted information derived from these 'other realms' and in that sense her work was doubly abstract. It was an abstraction not only in this world but also from some other world, or worlds. It was as if information had poured through a membrane impervious to the rest of us, but porous to af Klint. When her younger sister Hermina died in 1880, Hilma became interested in spiritualism, which was also fashionable at the time, and this in turn led her to the ideas of Madame Blavatsky, the founder of the Theosophical Society. Af Klint joined the Stockholm Lodge of the Theosophical Society on 23 May 1904 and she attended the Theosophical World Congress held in Stockholm in June 1913. The society has three main objects: to form a nucleus of the universal brotherhood of humanity, regardless of race, creed, sex, caste or colour; to encourage the comparative study of religion, philosophy, and science; and to investigate unexplained laws of nature and the powers latent in humanity. In addition, Blavatsky cautioned theosophists to trust only their own judgement on all questions, and to take nothing on trust, including anything she, herself, might say. The abstract works of Hilma af Klint embody many important theosophical ideas - the sevenfold constitution of human consciousness, reincarnation, and the unity of all life, the idea that everything is one thing, that the universe is a single unit from electron to gas giant.

My own subjective experience of practising as an artist suggests that ideas sometimes appear spontaneously and fully formed. It is as if they have been transmitted rather than created. They do indeed seem to 'flow through' from some other realm and the manner of transmission is rarely clear. Sometimes I 'simply know' how to move forward with my own work without understanding the source of that 'knowing'. In these instances ideas arrive complete and of a piece. Nothing needs to be added or taken away. They simply have to be executed. On other occasions works have to be fought for, or pieced together one fragment at a time, and these ideas always feel far more 'man made' as a consequence and less 'revealed'. I've often wondered if there is a qualitative difference between the ideas derived in these two very different ways, but there doesn't seem to be as far as I can tell. What is hard won and put together piecemeal can add up to something just as whole and satisfying as works that were 'revealed' suddenly, and in their entirety.

In *Lucid Between Bouts of Sanity*, an artist's manifesto about deeper expressive potential (Providence Press, 1996), I wrote, 'It is impossible to become lucid by degrees: the slightest fragmentary glimpse lays bare the entire terrain.' Perhaps something like the theosophical idea of involution is involved in these 'revealed' works.

Theosophy maintains that involution is the process by which the spiritual enters into the physical realm. Involution allows the divine to form itself into the material cosmos and infuse every aspect of it with spiritual insight.

When artistic ideas appear spontaneously perhaps some form of 'spiritual insight' has found its way into the quotidian world through the hands of the artist. Perhaps the artist is the medium for a localised involutionary effect. Hilma af Klint wrote in her notebook of her own works: 'The pictures were painted directly through me, without any preliminary drawings, and with great force. I had no idea what the paintings were supposed to depict; nevertheless I worked swiftly and surely, without changing a single brush stroke.'

Af Klint had been chosen by the High Masters to create the paintings for the 'Temple' though she was never entirely clear what the 'Temple' was, or might be. There are 193 Temple paintings in total. The major paintings from 1907 are very large, measuring approximately 240cm x 320cm. This series of pictures, The Ten Largest, depicts the different phases of life, from early childhood to old age. Once she had finally completed the works for the Temple, she felt that her spiritual guidance had ended, the period of local involuntary action was over, and she was left once again to her own devices. She continued to paint independently, but often on a much smaller scale, using water colour.

In her will, Hilma af Klint stipulated that her work should be kept secret for at least 20 years after her death. This indicates that she understood the revolutionary or even subversive nature of what she had been able to accomplish. It's also said that she knew her work would be incomprehensible in her own time. The boxes that contained her oeuvre were eventually opened at the end of the 1960s.

No One Knows
What Is Really Important

In 1970, af Klint's entire collection of paintings was offered as a gift to Moderna Museet in Stockholm. To its very great discredit, the museum declined to take her pictures. Something similar occurred when the Museum of Modern Art (MOMA) in New York refused to help Peggy Guggenheim move her art collection from Venice to the US for safekeeping during World War II. (The entire collection was eventually relocated at her own expense, travelling in the hold of a cargo ship, uninsured, along with other people's cookers, vacuum cleaners, beds, pots and pans.) Later, when MOMA wanted to show The Peggy Guggenheim Collection, Peggy was keen to take up their offer of making a speech at the vernissage. She took great delight in repeating the museum's original assessment that her collection was simply not important enough to warrant their help.

Thanks to the more visionary art historian Åke Fant, Hilma af Klint's art was introduced to an international audience in the 1980s, when he presented her work at a Nordic conference in Helsinki in 1984. Perhaps the times had caught up with af Klint to a degree, particularly given the gains made by feminism in the 1960s and 70s bringing greater respect and scholarship to the work of women writers and artists. Hilma's heir, Erik af Klint, donated thousands of drawings and paintings to The Hilma af Klint Foundation in the 1970s. Astonishingly, af Klint's artistic legacy includes more than 1,200 abstract paintings. It's tempting to note similarities between Hilma af Klint and Peggy Guggenheim in that they were each, in their day, women making waves in a male-centric world. Perhaps their pictures were deemed less significant precisely because they were created and championed by women, and women were regarded as being incapable of serious critical judgement in those times. It feels equally significant that theosophy's most significant figure is a woman in the form of its redoubtable founder, Madame Helena Petrovna Blavatsky. It feels significant too that the other essay in this volume is written by a woman, Madame Pogosky (Aleksandra Loginovna Pogosskaia) who, in her own field, was equally independent, innovative and prominent. These points are important because our culture needs figures who are able and willing to open up new spaces of potential. It is counter-productive for a culture to limit itself by only taking seriously the work of one half of the population. It is clear that af Klint's High Masters were more enlightened creatures in that they spoke to women in preference to men on many occasions. The same can be said of theosophy's 'Masters of Wisdom', the enlightened initiates who chose to communicate their insights to Madame Blavatsky. What other women might have contributed to these new potentials had they not been suppressed, denied or lost? It's interesting, and sobering, to ask the question how much poorer is our culture artistically and spiritually than it needs to be?

The surrealist movement, led by André Breton in Paris in the early 20th Century, was dominated by men but perhaps one of the most important surrealist works was made by a woman. Méret Oppenheim, a German-born Swiss artist, created 'Le déjeuner en fourrure', a fur covered teacup, saucer and teaspoon, known in English as 'Breakfast in Fur', in 1936. This famous work is said to be the result of a conversation in a café between Oppenheim and Picasso in which he suggested there were all kinds of things that were improved by being covered in fur. To this reasonably explicit come-on, Oppenheim replied with the sharper put-down, 'Even this cup and saucer?' The comment was doubtlessly intended to deflate Picasso's sexism, but it also birthed one of surrealism's most recognisable and distinctive objects. 'Le déjeuner en fourrure' was the first artwork by a woman acquired by MOMA for its permanent collection.

The surrealist interest in dreams and the unconscious has a particularly theosophical ring to it. In theosophical thought, dreams take place on the astral plane, a parallel realm of existence where our astral bodies experience astral realities. Memories of these astral occurrences impinge on our physical existences as the memories of dreams. Much of surrealism was the attempt to give physical expression to these experiences lived out on the astral plane. It was believed that artistic truth could express the profounder 'astral truth' of dreams. In a rather pleasing twist of fate, Méret Oppenheim's first retrospective in 1967 was hosted by Moderna Museet Stockholm, the very same organisation that was to turn down the gift of af Klint's body of work. By this time, surrealism was universally understood as an important movement in the history of 20th-century art. (af Klint's work was far more mysterious, unfamiliar and arcane. As a woman and a theosophist, af Klint clearly stretched the critical faculties of the museum's curatorial team too far.) On 16 January 1975, Méret Oppenheim was honoured with the Art Award of the City of Basel. In her acceptance speech, she summed up her position, saying simply, 'Freedom is not given to you - you have to take it.'

Do Theosophists Make Better Artists?

The socialist realism art movement, the official art of the USSR, persisted as the communist-prescribed artistic style from 1932 to 1988. Socialist realism often produced unremarkable or lacklustre results, in my view, because it represented a closing down of possibility. Artists must be open to possibility. Art is a form of unpredictability. Once it becomes predictable it fails as art. Artists must 'take the freedom', as Méret Oppenheim put it, to try out ideas. They must be free to investigate 'space potentials' that do not yet exist. By 'space potentials' I mean new realms of realisation that currently exist in potential only. For example, no one could run the four-minute mile. It existed as a 'space potential' but it had never been realised. When Roger Bannister ran a mile in under four minutes, he realised that potential, not only for himself but for all athletes who have followed since and now commonly run the mile in less than four minutes. The human body did not change. Time did not change. But the realisation of the space potential changed what was possible. In some ways, all artists are looking for, and exploring, space potentials. They are investigating latent potential in themselves and their practice. And as we have already seen, one of the key objects of Blavatsky's Theosophical Society is to explore the potential latent in humanity. Not all theosophists are artists but perhaps all artists would benefit from being theosophists. Space potentials can only be found in freedom - in my case usually by experiment - so that the artistic impulse can flow into that space and populate it. What we believe may be possible is what becomes possible for us. This is to restate some of theosophy's central ideas about the concrete nature of thought. Mightn't crucial space potential be discovered through reckless freedom or a freeing recklessness (many artists have been drunk a lot of the time) or through rigorous intellectual activity, or through spiritual awareness or exploration? Why not? Who is to say the necessary space potential is not pre-existing somewhere beyond that usually non-porous membrane that Hilma af Klint seemed able to breach? If art is an enquiry into the nature of things, and into possibility, and into our relationship with the world around us, then art, itself, is theosophical.

Why Artists Are Revered

Just as the priesthood spent its time in contemplation of things that were different from the general population's daily preoccupations, so artists are engaged in an activity 'to one side of the rest of the world'. This difference quite literally sets the artist apart as a saint or hermit might be set apart (that is not to suggest that artists are saintly, but they are usually different). Mental health challenges, anxieties and addictions are common. The artist's openness brings with it specific challenges. The attempt at porosity to other modes of existence and perceptual planes is a dangerous endeavour.

When af Klint found a way to receive information from other realms she also made herself vulnerable to the mental disturbance that might be caused by involuntary forces. There is an element of asceticism in this attempt at 'knowing by receiving' and there is no doubt in my mind that opening these doors-of-transmission can be deleterious to the human person. Artists need appreciation not criticism. The work is hard, often poorly paid and fraught with risk.

Art and Socialism

In my own practice, art and social equality, fairness and more equitable social organisation are closely linked. I believe that my work can have a degree of utility, opening up space potential for a kinder and more humane world. Ideas have a life. Thought has form. These are canonical theosophical ideas. Presenting ideas in public space may change that space and that public. Just as the four-minute mile changed athletics, so might often repeated ideas about equality and compassion change society. If you can catalyse debate, change usually follows.

Theosophy recognises the principles of universal brotherhood and the unity of all life. According to theosophy everything partakes of life and all life is interconnected and one. These are also distinctly socialist ideas. Annie Besant, the

Theosophical Society's second president was also a prominent figure in British socialism. For me art, socialism and theosophy are intertwined.

The other text in this volume, Madame Pogosky's essay *The International Union of Arts and Crafts*, is closely connected with Marxist socialist ideas. She calls for the 'free possession of the land by the tiller of it'. She describes the plight of hand embroiderers and lace-makers who work from home, prey to 'middlemen' who exploit peasant workers whilst being themselves incapable of embroidery or lace-making.

The Russian War Office ordered large quantities of embroidery for use on military uniforms - numbers and symbols indicating position and rank. This created many opportunities for middlemen to sweat the embroiderers until a member of the County Council decided to investigate workers' pay and conditions. The Councillor took it upon himself to visit the War Office and acquire an order for embroidery. He then established cooperative working practices and paid each worker a fair wage. When profits turned out to be higher than expected, he was able to increase each embroiderer's income, again through profit sharing. According to Pogosky, 'He gave directions to add something like 50% to the former scale of payment.' And she adds, 'It shows how much could be done, even under the present commercial conditions of the labour market.'

Capitalism is problematic because it withdraws capital from society, concentrating it into smaller and smaller circles of ownership where it can have no further social utility. Today's large corporations are so engorged with capital they have nowhere to spend it. Meanwhile, the poor struggle to meet their own basic needs for food and shelter. Any thinking person must be ethically troubled by these very great inequalities. There is enough food to feed all the hungry in the world but capitalism will not do it, simply because it cannot be done profitably. The starving cannot pay. To give food away would destabilise the market. Profit would be lost. The fact that people are starving is a direct consequence and cost of capitalism. Late-stage capitalism is like a game of Monopoly where one player is winning decisively. Eventually the winner's money must be redistributed amongst the other players or the game itself will grind to a halt. When the winner holds all the wealth, the game ends, everything stops.

Art and Money

Madame Pogosky was a progressive and most likely a feminist, in action if not in name. She is concerned for the welfare of the piece-workers and craftswomen she describes. 'Money is well taken care of. It is only the world's handicrafts, whatever their magnitude, that are neglected, uncared for, because they run in separate efforts.' She is concerned about collective action for justice. The question of money in Pogosky's essay is a question of fair reward for work done. She writes, 'Help is wanted in protection of the craftsman in this dangerous passage from work, as a natural expression of Spirit, to work meaning the manufacturing of goods in order to earn money.' Pogosky is careful to make a distinction between spiritual activity and commercial activity, even though there may appear to be a surface similarity.

It is true, of course, that we live in a capitalist system. In this system the value of something is necessarily measured by its market value. If art is to be valued in the current system it must have a monetary value. But in my opinion this fiscal value must always operate as a side issue. Art itself has nothing to do with money. Value is not created by the market but by the artist. Art is essentially a spiritual undertaking and you cannot monetise spiritual worth. There is something of inherent value about a work of art that is not determined by outside forces. Art is the sole province of artists.

It is immoral to work in the relative comfort and affluence of an advertising agency, for example, and claim to be an artist. It is tantamount to the City trader claiming to be a saint. Art can only ever be in service to its own aims. Anything in service to a third party is necessarily not art.

This is one of the reasons that art and artists cannot be censored. Censorship is always a failure because it relies on the moral judgement of the censor which will never accord absolutely with the moral judgement of the population. The water is muddied even further because morality is a constantly changing characteristic of culture. It flexes over time. One man's obscenity becomes another man's light reading. 'A glimpse of stocking is something shocking.' Until it isn't any more. If art is in service to anything other than its own aim (an 'official' style like socialist realism, a censor, or money) it is no longer the pure thing, art. It has become commercial art, advertising, or propaganda.

There are no doubt artists who will disagree with this assessment. Many successful careers have been built by careful observation of the art market and the creation of artworks that will sell. Whatever is 'made for market' is bound to have a degree of short term success.

Virginia Woolf pointed out that a novel by her friend Vita Sackville-West would out-sell her own novel *The Waves* ten-to-one. But history confirms that the greater artistic value lies in Woolf's work. A young writer once asked the great American experimentalist Gertrude Stein what he should do because he couldn't find a publisher. Her reply was simply to keep writing. She said publication was not something to be concerned about: the only important thing was to keep the writing 'coming out of you'. Stein, perhaps more than anyone, understood the idea that value and money were often only remotely, or sometimes never, connected. She was fortunate in that she had a private income. This enabled her to work independently and her independence allowed her great artistic clarity. She was able to work solely for the love of working, not for the prospect of financial reward.

Work Is Love

Pogosky writes 'work is love'. I don't believe she meant 'toil is love', but creative work, making things like embroidery or lace, can be an act of love. Like any love, this act of love cannot survive if it is part of a wider system of abuse. Pogosky saw that the love of work combined with equitable social organisation could produce the conditions under which human beings flourish. As the saying goes: 'Do something you love and you'll never do a day's work.'

But in Pogosky's view, when things go wrong it is because people have become disconnected from each other and feeling has failed: 'The workers, the leaders, the producers and the consumers do not love each other, do not know each other. They are groping in the dark, not knowing that they are limbs of one common body, under one common law, that they cannot do without each other.' The antidote is worker organisation and participation where power is shared, decisions are made jointly, leadership is diffuse and by consensus. In some ways these were the original hopes of the Russian revolution. There would be no party politics, only 'soviets' (the Russian word for 'councils') representing the interests of the people. There would be no elections because there would be no ruling party, only the will of the people. Sadly something went wrong along the way. Pogosky has the courage to suggest that perhaps it was nothing more complicated than the absence of love. This seems to me a particularly feminine perspective and I wonder if any of Pogosky's male peers would have been bold enough (or sufficiently insightful) to talk in these emotive terms.

Pogosky has to be admired for her independence of thought, her moral and emotional courage, and her modernity. She was fiercely internationalist and believed in the self-organisation of creative workers as a powerful force for good. She writes, 'In Russia... the rulers find it undesirable to allow the union of various workers, as they know only too well that Union is Strength.' Madame Pogosky suggests that with greater social justice, the work of the embroiderers, the lace-makers and all creative people can become love made visible once again.

At the heart of the theosophical impulse is the belief in brotherhood and the interconnectedness of all life. In so many ways theosophy has been, and remains ahead of its time. Where work is organised for the benefit of all, love can also take up residence. A work of art is no different. A work of art that calls for greater social justice has the potential to implicate all of society rather than being the preserve of a self-selecting museum-going class or cultural elite. Public art is inherently participative. I have always felt that to make a work of art, or even simply to have the intention to make art, is itself a form of loving. For me art is essentially theosophical because it describes some form of operation of the spirit, some stretching up of our shared humanity in recognition of itself.

A. L. Pogosky

Aleksandra Loginovna Pogosskaia, A. L. Pogosky, or Madame Pogosky (1848-1921) was a Russian emigre, an activist and business woman promoting Russian art in the West. Her first foray into selling Russian handicrafts was in New York in the early 1890s where she was the manager of a retail outlet at 130 East 23rd Street called Russian Cottage Industries.

By 1900 she had moved to Britain and established her own Russian Peasant Industries depot in Bond Street, selling Russian embroideries, textiles, furniture, toys, and illustrated books of Russian folk tales. Besides her retail outlets, she also organised selling exhibitions, touring towns in England and Scotland. Her promotion of the work of Russian peasant artisans included a concern for the working conditions of women in lace-making and she became a vocal champion of socially responsible business.

Madame Pogosky became a member of the Theosophical Society in 1909 after attending the society's summer school in Norfolk that year. She was drawn to the society's object of forming a 'universal brotherhood of humanity' and applied this idea to communal work in the arts. A socialist approach to artistic production would enable peasant artisans to become self-organising and self-supporting. She was the founder of The International Fellowship of Workers and in 1913 she set out the principles of her new arts and crafts organisation in a polemical tract, *Fellowship in Work*, published in Russian under the title *The Ideals of Labour as the Basis for a Happy Life*.

In her final years she returned to Russia and died at a theosophical commune in the city of Kaluga, 150km southwest of Moscow.

The International
Union of Arts and Crafts
by A. L. Pogosky (1917)

Part One

In all ages, in all countries, everywhere where life is, work is, was, and ever will be the eternal expression of man, his eternal function of service. Some may be conscious of it, some may not. Some may seek in it the most sacred outlet for the soul to reach God, and then we have the creation of such works as the divine heirlooms of masters, in pictures, poems, sculptures; some may take to work instinctively as one who has thirst takes a drink of water, whether it is handed to him in a crystal vessel, or whether he has to bend over a brooklet like that very simple inhabitant of the woods - the young goat or the wood pigeon. Some, again, in their instinctive longing to fulfil their function, obediently bend their neck under the yoke of heavy labour, like a willing horse or ox.

All these differences do not hide from the thinker the deep significance of one great idea of human life, the greatest, the most sacred - work.

Long, aye, too long, have we been ignoring this. We have been toying with it, perverting its very foundation into every possible shape; under what we are pleased to call our social conditions, we have made it an object of barter, a means of injustice and cruelty, a means of subjugation and degradation.

Truly depressing is the contemplation of all the tragic sights which surround us at present, the problems of labour which baffle the clearest minds. But there is a great hope which manifests itself daily in human life: no sooner does a man form an earnest decision to seek for truth, to re-establish the broken law, than a great transformation scene ensues, misery becomes joy, the most difficult problems become as clear as daylight.

Anyone who has gone through the second birth - call it what you will - or who has, after a toilsome life of disharmony, fruitless efforts and struggles, at last found himself, knows and knows well how, when the true law is found and re-established in life - in spite of the required sacrifice of those sides of life which we are brought up to consider as the true and desirable ends of life - it works wonders; how the frowns of the depressed, miserable toiler smooth away into gladness and joy; how distrust, suspicion, even hatred, turn into love and welcome; how every new day, instead of being a weary sigh, is welcomed by a joyous leap of the grateful heart.

So let us consider these important matters together; let us follow the threads one by one, trying to find where the tangle began; let us unite in one joyful band of seekers after truth, after the law of work, of life; let us unite all men and women of all nations, of all creeds; let us help each other in the supreme task of regeneration; here is a task, indeed, which wants the union of all temperaments., all histories, all races, all experiences. Such a band has already been formed - on the 9th July 1910 - into a nucleus of workers, and is sending this message to all brothers and sisters in work throughout the world: join us and help us to find truth.

Shall we speak of the modern state of all the aspects of work? Is it not the sorest of sores of every thinker, of every lover of humanity? Why, the very toiler would laugh in our face if we dared to state the simple truth: work must be one with love. Yet if we think of an example of good, useful, or gifted and inspired work, we cannot help seeing that this is true. The artist who expresses his best in his 'work' loves it. The peasant who walks after the plough loves the field, the horse co-worker, the bird which flutters round the newly opened furrow, the sky and sun overhead, the brooklet which refreshes his tired body; he loves the vision of his heavily loaded sheaves in the near future, the very smell of the earth and its fruit.

The philosopher, who for years and years accumulates new arguments and aspects of his idea which he gives to the world, does not grudge the many years his work of love and devotion will take; he loves his idea too well to robe it in indifferent clothing; he wants it as beautiful, as magnificent, as transparent, as it appears to him in his moments of ecstasy and illumination.

The work of a woman is the endless expression of her love and devotion in its many aspects, in its many varieties of degrees according to her own development; it falls as low as the simple providing of food and comfort for the bodily wants of her beloved ones; it rises often as high as heaven in meeting the spiritual needs of those she brought into the world, inspiring them with lofty ideals and virtues.

Let us look a little further, and observe the modern development of this all-important function.

The artist who no longer seeks to express himself, because he has to sell the pictures, and his ideal may not please the buyer - aye, may even, by waking the conscience of the moneyed buyer, inspire unpleasant feeling and revulsion - instead of lovingly clothing his idea and handing it lovingly to the world, has to lower himself in order to please, has to hand it to the public with a curse and hatred, because of his own lowering, his own degradation.

The musician, who, in his upward path, heard the angels sing, who himself kept the heavenly harmonies stored in his best self, appears on the public platform. The common ear of the profane cannot hear the subtle, heavenly strains. It is overhung with ostrich feathers, overwhelmed with worldly gossip and selfconsciousness; so the musician has to accomplish sensational feats of musical gymnastic, overtop his predecessor, make a 'record' of musical 'performance' to reach this common ear. There is no love lost between these again. There cannot be, as for the sake of this audience the heavenly strains must be forgotten, ignored. Where is the one who walked after his plough, inhaling the bitter-sweet smell of Mother Earth, basking and sweating under the summer sun, dreaming of his golden crop ? Where is he now? Alas! You find him the slave of a machine, no more a poet nor a creator of crops and beauty, no more in direct contact with Isis, but depressed, defiled, pale and small-hearted, afraid of the next day, bitter and cursing his fate, when after his day's work he returns 'home' not unlike one of those 'clinkers' rolled into waste among ashes, all the life taken out of him. No love, to be sure, here, no expression of his individual divine Self, no present, no future, even no past to lovingly remember.

The scholar, the writer - where is he? Where are those many who, like millions of seeds, are shaken over the earth by liberal divine hands, to spread life and beauty into every corner of our earth? Alas! We find them again and again drudging away, living only with part of their hearts and minds, ignoring their best Selves, giving what they have to give only for money, educating often a new taste for what is low and demoralising. For our own demoralisation must spread, must tell on all we touch. Blessed are those who carry their real light through all difficulties. Those are they who will save humanity.

How did the trouble begin? When was the law broken? Every corner of the world has its own history of this Fall. And this is one point where we, the Fellows of the International Union of Workers, may help each other. Let the Irish worker tell us when, and under what influence, the expression of his celtic soul ceased to be a natural outlet for his individual gifts, and became an object of barter. Let the Hindu tell us when his hour of degradation came, and what brought it on. When did the grand lines of his creative architects change into the mean 'modern style', no longer a symbol of his soul, beliefs and aspirations? When did it happen, for the first sad time, that the maiden came to the well holding on her shoulders not the classical, curved earthen vessel, but - horror of all horrors - a tin kerosene can? When were the noble, flowing garments of hand-spun and woven web of soft hues exchanged for cotton, machine-made rags of the vilest colours? When we find the cause and the time of these changes in history, we shall also have found the cause of the loss of love in Work, and the point to which we shall have to return again, and to direct our efforts to start afresh, with a wisdom aided by long years of experience. Let the Russian tell us how he lost the love of Work, so evidently manifested in every fragment of ancient work, of which the country is still overfull. No, not even very ancient. Not so many years ago there was no pair of hands, among the peasants at least, which could not express itself in many ways, in weaving and embroidery, in carving and modelling - express itself in a language sanctified by tradition, by beliefs, and by the memory of their ancient eastern cradle. Some are yet living, and still creating beauty.

The dwellers of the towns lost all this, simply by turning their faces away from traditions, from deserted, defiled churches, from their own history. There was a new craving for western civilisation. No price seemed too high to pay for this semblance of culture.

The peasant lost his old love for his work in another way. Daily and hourly came the wily thief nearer to the door; money was heeded for causes foreign to his interest. Money was needed badly for war, for keeping in subjugation the Russian frontiers, frontiers encircling millions and millions of acres which peasants dared not touch, dared not transform into a garden of life, of golden crops, of happiness for all. Money was also badly wanted for keeping up thousands and thousands of tax-collectors, hard taskmasters, excise officials, controllers, a whole army of oppressors. It was also needed for building expensive official buildings, where an army of clerks were busy writing unnecessary papers and smoking unnecessary cigarettes all day long. It was needed to build expensive buildings for official Science, presided over by docile scholars, dispensing their dead facts to the youths of the towns.

What did the worker of the fields, the poet of the hills, dales, rivers and lakes, know of all this? Nothing whatever! But in his humble way, in his habit of obedience to forces beyond his small self, he bent his neck lower and lower, he increased his efforts more and more, he got panic stricken sometimes with all the misery, and the needs, and the neglect of his fellow men, he who had no time to think, to rest, to take better care of his body, of his home and children, while working unceasingly to satisfy those mysterious needs claimed by his betters!

In olden times, he was a free man. He lived unmolested in God's own garden, he lovingly tended it, deriving from its beautiful fruit all he needed. The golden crops of grain and seeds, the cream white potatoes, the rich dark green multitudes of cucumbers, the red apples of his garden, the wild, abundant berries of all kinds and colours, sweet and sour, all life giving and all pleasant to gather, and all the other numerous gifts of the woods and hills, of rivers, and lakes - these fed him and his little ones, and he 'ate his bread in thankfulness'.

The silky green flax with the delicate little blue flowers, rolling down the slopes of his fields to the cool water-fed dales, like a rich carpet woven by elves and fairies, lovingly clad him, his wife, his mother, and his children; and, in the hands of the woman under the rays of the eternal sun, became as white and as pure as snow. The little flowers of the fields and meadows, the fantastical patterns of Father Frost on the small windows in the winter, all the harmonies of foliage, hues, and moods of Isis, enveloped by woman's love in mystic lore, nursed through the nights of free communion with Nature in her simple peasant life, working and eating, loving and sleeping in the open air under the ever-mysterious starry heaven - all this was told by her in clever artistic adornments of garments, wrought in colours and symbols, more felt than known as a science. She would wander out into the woods and hunt for the sweet-smelling heather and the bitter, refreshing, pungent birch leaf, and dig for the red-hearted madder and pluck the yellow golden daisy. The red was like her idea of glory. Where could she direct it but to the Almighty God presiding above? The yellow daisy was the pure gold of her simple aspirations, the flame of her heart, like the flame of the taper in church, lifting her on its fiery tongues to the Unspeakable. And the blue of the cornflower, was it not like her humble devotion So what wonder that these gifts of God's garden were crystallized into vegetable dyes, since ever one remembers man's life. All round about the peasant home man was surrounded by symbols of Isis; he read a meaning into the lofty trees and the mysterious flowers which open only for a single night; he saw things in the woods which no one else saw; he heard from his cradle of unseen forces of Nature, of mysterious beings - helpers and foes, some whom he feared, some whom he learnt to obey. It was a constant union and intermixing of real life with legends of ancient time; it was the Russian Frost born from the prehistoric eastern cradle. Else how could a pomegranate appear on a peasant's towel? The modern scholar reads the pomegranate as a symbol of royalty; and so it might be. But the Hindu's reading of it as an emblem of sorrow, as a tear, seems more real, more likely; and this is why a pomegranate is always borne before a funeral procession.

The birds? All those feathery flocks of so many hues and voices, how did they affect the peasant imagination? Surely they were the most mysterious beings on earth. Ever since the Aryan race began, the birds have been the embodiment of thoughts and messages; they were the souls of the departed. Thousands of legends, one more beautiful than the other, live even now in the memory of peasants. Their lore is full of graceful suggestions in this direction. So what more natural than to carve the beloved symbol in wood and metal, to work it in iron and silver, silk and thread? Even now, in our twentieth century, one can find in every village and home - far enough away from a railway's levelling influence - birds carved at every end of the huge rafters, or looking down from the top of the roof, or two peacocks (symbols of life eternal) adorning an over window, usually turned face to face towards the 'Tree of Life'. The bird shapes itself as a curious utensil, daily in use on the peasant table - the salt cellar. It runs in joyous bands or Indian file over the borders of tablecloth and bed clothes, hangs down from towels, and adorns every church curtain. It looks out mysteriously from the folds of the ancient brocade gown, and shines in golden threads over the woman's face.

Even now, in the twentieth century, if one takes the trouble to go out of the beaten track to some northern peasant home - perhaps getting a bed in a little attic, called in Russia a 'light room', and finding a collection of ancient garments on the wall, under a blue linen cover - one is struck with all this living history of human life, thought and symbolism, all the hidden, unspoken beauty of a poet's heart. It is a revelation! Every stitch seems to be put in with a blessing, with a smile, put as a mother puts the last touch to her little darling's attire, lovingly, gently. Aye, those people felt beauty. They loved to wear beautifully made garments; they seemed never to have grudged the time nor the efforts to make every piece of clothing a true poem. It suited so well the home, the field, the work. The elaborate making of it suited the long winter evenings. It was an elevation of the soul to follow the ancient religious symbols, like an all-day prayer, needed in those dark winter days, when the joyous sun shows so little and the soul is obscured through the wintry, narrow conditions. It was also a reminiscence of the splendid summer work among the green fields and fragrant trees and flowers, among all those bright colours with which a maiden likes to surround herself. No wonder this winter work was always made in social gatherings and accompanied with songs. All life then was a fairy tale, all fairy tales were life. They were one.

And now for the stealthy approach of the thief, the enemy, the destroyer of all this picturesque life?

How obnoxious a task to write a history of destruction! Yet it is necessary, as there are many yet who do not see the fiend under the mask of 'civilisation', 'improvement', 'growth of industry', 'accumulation of a nation's wealth'. A modern destroyer must be attractive, or else he could not succeed. He came very softly; he imitated one who wished well, wished light and happiness.

At first he brought machines. Thousands found work in those new factories. Fathers and brothers and husbands went there first.

It seemed hard to part for years, hard for the women to do all the men's work besides their own; it seemed hard never to hear from them, ever expecting a thunder message of death or accident, to dream of broken ties, of temptations; but more and more efforts were made. Then they returned, those first pioneers.

Ah! In what a strange way! Changed to a degree! Nothing in the village was good enough; their very wives and sweethearts no more lovable and desirable - only stupid village folks. The simple fare, the bast shoes, the sober daily work - all this was stupid. Earnings? Yes, some brought nearly enough to pay the taxes, hardly enough to pay the damage caused by the lack of the man's share in work. And then they all wanted to show off; they had to buy in town modern garments, and walk through the street with the new-fangled harmonica, and shout in a half-drunken voice the new 'fashionable' songs inspired by the factory. Ah well, it was almost a blessing when the short holidays ended and the men returned to their factories again. But the seed was planted. Soon after, women found their way to the factories. Who knows where the call came from? Whether from the bits of town finery, in which the country maiden thought she looked 'almost like a lady'; or from the great hunger for freedom, for her own sweet will; or the mysterious attraction of a new, unknown life, the breaking down of old traditions, new ways, new clothes, a new moral code altogether. So women followed men. Most of them found more than they had bargained for. They lived a hell of a life; these healthy country flowers soon fell an easy prey to the towns. Who was there to protect and love them for their own sake, to respect their womanhood and motherhood? Huddled together were men, women, and maidens, all together in a heap of misled humanity, no one to give compassion, only to blame and condemn! How could it be otherwise? Intolerably long hours, low pay, unexpected fines, a mysterious grinding and pressing of all there was in them of life, womanhood, truth. All ground together, exhausted and thrown out - a factory's 'waste'. What was the effect of this second exodus on the village life?

More exhaustion, more hopelessness, more despair, less and less strength in work. And then, after years, the debauched, diseased, exhausted wanderers came home one by one, to sponge on the remainder of the family, to curse and drink an ignoble death, leaving consternation and dumb suffering behind.

What then has to be done to re-establish justice manhood, happiness, poetry of life? Can we not see the broken law? What is there to do but to give the peasant - wherever he may live, on the shores of the Volga, or of the sacred Ganges, in the Highlands of Scotland, or in the Emerald Isle - the land; the free possession of the land by the tiller of it?

I hear many, many voices violently calling me a Utopian, a madcap. How can this be, where the State must be the legal owner, and the regulation of the laws? How very unpractical to wish an artist, preacher, a musician, a writer, to give their best for the sake of service! How can they live? They will perish of starvation. Absurd and ridiculous!

Aye, friends, I am only one of you. I have no magic means to accomplish miracles, but the Truth I have. If we aim at truth, happiness, love, we must make sacrifices, every one of us, rich and poor, influential and humble. We must supply the conditions for the miracle to happen. We must nurse this ideal deep in our hearts; forget the buying and selling of our spiritual gifts; give, give freely as it was given to us freely, and lovingly. Only then shall we hear real music, see inspired works of art, see happy faces, and the colossal army of unemployed receding into the dark pages of history. Only then will our daily life become heaven.

I hear also a few half-sympathetic voices of those who have long thought the same thoughts, nursed the same ideals. This golden age may come, I hear them say, but after many generations, after long evolution of mankind; neither we nor our children and grand-children may see it accomplished.

Against this let me plead. Truly, if we and our children will for ever remain passive, feebly folding our hands before the great task, sinking down at the roadside in a hopeless despair, then indeed can we have no hope of conquering the dragon which we have created by ourselves by this very indolence and self-indulgence. The time is ripe for rising up against the evil, so as not to let it get more and more the better of us. Is it not bad enough as it is? Shall we wait for more and more suffering to be sent to us to bring us to our senses, to our duty?

And then, is not all this misery really only a bogey? Take to pieces the greatest of modern evils, the injustice of one being sick and helpless from overwhelming richness, the other sick and helpless from lowest poverty. What is it all made of? Simply ignorance, greediness, selfishness. There is really no organic impossibility of re-establishing justice. As soon as we realise what Brotherhood is, we shall feel revulsion against our own crime, then the only solution, no longer difficult but desirable and lovable, will be to give up all unearned privileges, to share, to give, to be one of the Brothers.

Let us begin in a very small way, in little groups of Justice and Service. Let us unite in these efforts wherever we happen to live, and do our duty to our neighbours. One of these groups has been started by the International Union of Workers on the 9th July, 1910.

Part Two

We are going to speak of practical details this time. Let us speak of them, then, but keep in view that all reform, all justice must be stated from within, as it is the Spirit that dictates and shapes matter, not matter that influences Spirit.

In this paper we are going to consider the means by which under present conditions we may bring some fresh breezes of the waking consciousness of the sanctity of work into some corners of its sphere at least, may consider whether it be not possible by love and wisdom, by devoted efforts and international interest, to create and supply conditions for a miracle of happy work to happen. One may call it compromise. Perhaps after ages of suffering we may take even this humbly, if by it, one can better even the minutest particle of existing evils.

It is a matter of temperament. Some form principles and theories for good things to come to humanity, somewhere, sometime; never seeming to claim the realisation of these good things at once, under their very eyes, brought about and helped by their very hands. Have we yet begun living our lofty ideals? I think not. Have you ever seen an earnest, strong-willed man or woman who did not succeed in shaping the circumstances of life sooner or later in his own way? If this is not true, then all the theories about 'thought is a deed', or 'thoughts are things', are childish dreams. So there is plenty of hope for us, who are ready to give our efforts, our lives, if need be, to establish the forgotten truth: Work and Love are one. If we are earnest we shall succeed, no matter how many mistakes we make on our way, nor how many thorny paths we may have to walk through.

Just at this moment we will not touch in any way the work of artists, musicians, writers, poets, or preachers. The tangle before our eyes is too big, too motley. And also we believe earnestly that those who, like them, come nearer than any of us to God on the wings of their gifts, are already thinking these thoughts themselves, and preparing a grand epoch of momentous importance, all tending to the same goal.

We shall dwell in our minds among those more humble workers, who toil and fret in all corners of the earth, toil so unceasingly that they almost forget their former freedom, are almost hopeless of brighter days. In this state of hopeless despair, brought about by ages of disharmony and injustice, by a broken law of equanimity, the toiler has no more time nor energy to think, to create, to fight. Someone must intervene, must take his cause to heart, must plead, must find the way where help lies, must take his suffering as his own. If this be done, half of the evil will recede. When we hear of the 'idle poor', of their improvidence, of their vices and dirty habits, we get into a tangle, we suffer and are lost in controversies. What should we say of a doctor who, finding a patient showing symptoms of typhus, cholera, or any other dangerous disease, should get hysterical and run away so as not to see such awful things? What are dirty habits, improvidence and all the rest of it among the poor, but symptoms of a more dangerous disease, which originated ages ago and is eating humanity away like cancer? It was brought about by ignorance and injustice, and the selfishness of men. Yet we pronounce it God's curse and run away, so as not to suffer ourselves from the sight of these symptoms. We allow children and younger men and women to fall into the same pit of horrors!

The disease has many symptoms, many degrees of development. At some of its stages, one can see plainly how a well-regulated hygienic treatment may bring to the patient recovery, comparative health and strength.

There are very numerous centres of handicrafts, for instance, in France in the Valley of the Rhone. The petites industries - what are called cottage industries in England - are reigning supreme there. They are little noticed by the big world's press, it is true, but it is a little world of its own. If you were to spend one of your holidays there, and decide upon a good walking tour through the sunny, smiling valley of the Rhone, from village to village, leaving behind hurry and worldly conception of time, just giving yourself up to the present joy of life and movement, entering into this new rural world with an open heart and keen observing eyes, you soon would find as much as did once a famous traveller, Ardouin Dumazet - to whose twenty-seven volumes I may refer those who like to investigate further. Every village seems to have its own characteristics, its own sounds and ways. In some of them folks are making pipes, nothing but pipes of sweet briar; in others violins, and then you see the idea of the violin in all stages of evolution, everywhere up to the very roofs, drying, bleaching, ripening and what not. Further we find a little factory, which produces only one shapeless thing in great masses - celluloid. And round it a group of villages shaping this mass into all sorts of elegant or useful things too numerous to mention. And we hear of a peaceful evening, when the father rests in his garden among his little ones, watering his flowers and peas, and looking happy and independent.

There are some groups of villages in Austria, the famous Zakopane district, where the old

Slavonia craft of wood-carving was brought from the ancient days of the Middle Ages right into the twentieth century. With the help of some of those idealists who could not succeed in losing their love for the beautiful, it took lately (some twenty to twenty-five years since) a fresh impetus, and the district is now covered with schools, and workshops, in fact has become a sight-seeing resort for tourists. The old traditions are sacredly kept by its leaders and teachers, but the twentieth century is clearly embodied in them, adding to the expression of the old Slavonic heart its new story of experiences. One need only go to the Church on Sunday and have a look at some young mother with her baby, to have a quaint picture of living history and symbolism. Whoever saw the fine, artistic, most elaborate garments of the baby, its little embroidered cap, every little detail of its clothing up to the richly embroidered, snow white cover (which truly should range among church embroidery), and the rosy, healthy face of the mother in her picturesque, snow white embroidered cap, would hardly believe such a thing could be yet in existence in our time of hurry and disharmony. Truly the eyes of men, women, and children, feeding, as they are even now, on beauty in nature, beauty in attire, and beauty in heart, are in a stage of development where they can be helped, where they must be helped. Is it absolutely necessary to have those graceful images broken, distorted and soiled, before they enter into a new cycle of progress? Could we not spare them the vulgarities of our so-called civilisation of today? Could we not be benefited ourselves by helping them through this stage of evolution, preserving all the best in the past, the traditions of excellent workmanship, up to the next rung of the ladder? Help is wanted in protection of the craftsman in this dangerous passage from work, as a natural expression of Spirit, to work meaning the manufacturing of goods in order to earn money, while land has become scarce and its tiller is obliged to take to some by-industry.

Under just conditions, which are bound to come when we alter our attitude into a just attitude of Brotherhood, the tiller of the land, having plenty of scope for his activity, will not need to produce 'goods' of any other kind but the greatest produce of all - the food of humanity, grain. And in the leisure time allowed to him while nature rests and gathers forces, he, obedient to his mother, will also rest and gather strength; all his practical gifts will come into play, and the experiences gathered through the summer's heavy work will flow freely through the functions of his intellectual gifts. This may find expression in many unexpected, heretofore undreamed of ways of beauty; because good seed in good conditions produces good fruit. We have forgotten the taste of such fruit, because we have made its growth a torture.

But I will take you now to some corners of the world in Russia, and show you some forms of industries.

Here is a small old town in central Russia. Its best street is not much of a street; a few brick houses, a few shops and bakeries, a market place with a good many deserted storehouses, a quaint, straggling little house or shed with the old-fashioned public scales, where on market days the peasants weigh their loads of grain, hay, and other produce when they are fortunate enough to dispose of them. This town is surrounded by a motley crowd of still smaller houses, some of them mere huts made of logs and covered with straw, radiating from the town limits in all directions along the roads into the country. These minute, insignificant looking, grey houses contain a larger population than the town itself. They belong to the so called burgher class. The little town stands on a brisk little river, and once was a centre of grain traffic; but the modern railway system shifted this centre to a new place, and the commercial significance of this little town collapsed; the storehouses were deserted, and the inhabitants of the suburbs, who used to get their living in a good many ways round about the once flourishing town, were left in desolation - no land, no earnings, no labour of any kind required any more.

In those days women saved the day. One by one they took to gold embroidery, and tapestry weaving, and leather work, led at first by nuns who had had this industry at their finger-ends for ages. Soon these church embroideries turned into a more democratic, widespread kind of goods, such as slippers, bags, cushions; the tapestry weavers made children's girdles and ties, also tapestry slippers and trimmings. The leather workers manufactured the same easily sold, useful goods in their own technique. The goods were bought and sold by ordinary drapers in large towns. Later, another element came in and added a new feature to the industry of this suburb, now largely known. The War Office gave large orders for embroidery devices, marks and numbers for different regiments, both for officers and men. Of course these new important orders were managed through middlemen, and carried on for many years without the public ever taking any interest in the matter. Even the nearest neighbours, even the local administration County Council never paid any attention to what was going on in the suburbs. The busy workers were there, their laborious lives also; one could not help seeing their faces bent over the frames, close to the small windows; the brilliant shops in the two capitals with all the showy, gold embroidered goods, so well known as Toryok industry, were before everybody's eyes. Yet no one ever tried to enter into the sphere of work, to learn how it was paid and managed. This indifference of the unthinking public is everywhere the best hotbed for sweating and degradation. This came to Toryok, nearer and nearer, and the coils of the sweating monster squeezed tighter and tighter, and the victims still clamoured for work.

Then a new era dawned upon the struggling workers. The first ray of compassion came from a good man, a member of the local Zemstvo. The thought suddenly dawned upon him that it was his duty to examine how those neighbours of his fared, how these units of taxation, levied by the very Zemstvos of which he was a member, were served. He went from house to house, and the information he obtained made him think, and think deeply. Why, it seemed as if he were plunged into hell itself, or into a very pit of crime, where the evil-doer went about at his own will, subjugating all under his own boot by the power of his money, and no one else had anything to say to it. It was the prerogative of the spider to entangle and suck the feebly moving fly.

The good man thought and thought, then he made a decision. He went to Petrograd and found a way to the War Office. Among the many thousands of big and small wheels and screws of this elaborate institution, he found at last the spring of the machinery. He gathered courage, obtained and signed a contract for so many embroidered marks and symbols for the various regiments, studied the designs and samples, obtained the materials and returned to his little old-fashioned Toryok. He engaged a young lady by the month to distribute the work among the embroiderers and receive and pay for it when finished. A new wheel was thus added to the activity of the local Zemstvo, a new field for study and justice - a real work of love, was it not?

The next few weeks and months were like the working of an immense beehive, with a new Queen. At the end of this period, the good man went to the War Office again, delivered the goods, received the money for them and signed a new contract for more work.

Then came an amazing surprise. There was far, far more money than what they paid to the workers. He calculated again and again, hardly believing in the possibility of such a gain. Then he gave directions to add something like 50% to the former scale of payment. The workers fervently crossed themselves, yet, old in experience, kept their joy in their own patient hearts. A few more months; another delivery of goods; still more surplus money coming; another rise of the wages; all this went on with progressing rapidity. In his official report, which I read with a beating heart at the great Exhibition of the Coronation Year, attached by a worn out cord to the splendid exhibits, the leader put it very quaintly: 'At last the wages reached 60 cop. a day (Is, 2d.), after which we considered them so abnormally high that we abstained from raising them any more and devised another plan of investment'. They organized a permanent department of cottage industries as part of the County Council's functions, took a house for the offices and stores, and started another branch - of lace-making, reviving, as they went along, the ancient designs from a rich collection of lace lovingly preserved by one who loved beauty. Just now, after eighteen years of steady progress, the centre has grown, and trained artists have contributed their efforts. At present these industries are in great demand all over Russia, and have a local wholesale depot. I do not mean to say that all the leading management is ideal and that no better ways could be found; yet I note this instance with gratefulness, because it shows how much could be done, even under the present commercial conditions of the labour market. It inspires hope, and works out some of the lines upon which the industries may be improved.

There is another corner of industries where darkness still reigns, where no loving heart yet sheds its life giving rays; therefore this garden of workdom stands with blighted, withered leaves, and flowers which have no power even to open - stands barren and desolate, It is a group of villages on the shores of the Volga, not far off the famous town of Nijni Novgorod. The shares of land allotted at the time of emancipation were very small, as is often the case where land is valuable (on the shores of large rivers, or the rich soil of Central Russia, for instance). The brisk traffic in these regions brought a more than usual increase of population, and the shares of land grew smaller and smaller, till at last only one of ten families could farm; the others had to take to some industries. Men took to boat-building, the majority sought earnings in other large towns, women alone remained at home. They were lace-makers for several generations. Every woman, old or young, every child from seven years old, made lace.

Middlemen, or rather a whole system of them, acted as distributors, enforced sweating, tightening the screw more and more. Cheaper, cheaper and cheaper, was the cry. The lace got looser and looser, it was handled in a disgraceful way, both parties vying with each other in getting the best bargain. It went on and on; the lace-makers earned less than the cost of bare rye bread. To the English ear it would sound incredible, but facts remain facts. A lace-maker could not earn more than one penny a day, working early and late. At last this cruel system over-reached itself, as all evil will. The lace became so bad that even cheap prices could not tempt any buyer, and the whole industry of many thousand workers collapsed.

Statistics never registered items of such dramas. Then these women and children lingered, sickened, died out - no one of the outside world ever knew, ever wished to know. During this period some of the more energetic women got occasional orders for some simple drawn-thread work. One or two earned some money at it. This sounded like a trumpet call. In a few weeks the drawn-thread work spread like smallpox. At every window one could see the bent down face of a woman over a frame. The middlemen reappeared. They came with very poor pay indeed, but even this was life. They required ready-made goods. The poorest could not afford to buy the yard of cotton stuff and spool of thread. Thus a new subdivision was organised. Some of the workers who could afford to invest a few shillings for materials, would take the order and give it out to the poorer workers at a lower price. Then there came a still more profitable system of sweating children. A woman sweater - a poor wretch herself - provides the material and starts the first, difficult part of the work herself, spreads large frames in her own house, and takes children to do the mechanical work. Only one kind of stitch all day long, with imperfect light from small windows, and all evening till late at night, with a poor, smoky kerosene lamp, from day to day, from month to month, from year to year, all life long - always the same, no variety. Bent over the frame, sitting sideways, so close together that only the right hand is free to move, with faces as white as paper and transparent like wax, these young martyrs of 'civilization' sit even today - yes, still stitching, stitching and stitching, and producing vile stuff in the shape of tea cloths, pillow-shams and d'oyleys, yet finding a market, not only in Russia, but even in Germany and England, because they are so very cheap.

Yet the very same women could be made to earn ten times more if some kind heart would take the trouble to provide protection and knowledge (Love and Wisdom). The middleman, as he exists now in Russia, can provide only a cheap market; he is unable to improve, to bring in ideas, to introduce better goods to a better class of buyers. He has only the coarsest methods and his only means is sweating.

I have no doubt that in every country similar causes and modern conditions must have similar results. We know something of sweating in England. From Dr. Coomaraswamy's excellent book, The Message of the East, one gathers the assurance of this being the case in India as well. But I give here illustrations from Russian industrial life, because I myself know it better and am hoping our international friends will add their experience. I will give another instance of certain efforts to improve conditions, this time from a north-east province of Russia - Viatka. A truly peasant province this, as on account of its severe climate there are very few noblemen's estates there, only the Tsar's forests and the peasants' shares of land. The members of the County Councils (Zemstvos) have to be elected mainly from the peasant communities. Let us see how it told on the management of peasant industries.

After Moskow, it was Viatka whose County Council led the movement and awoke to its duty first. The first contact with the requirements of the local industries (the territory of the province of Viatka exceeds Great Britain) showed the fact of total ignorance of the subject. One part of the province did not know the other, no one could tell what was manufactured and on what scale, which of the goods were consumed in their own province and which and on what scale were they exported to other markets. A few large sweating firms in the city of Viatka knew a thing or two, but kept quiet. Naturally enough the Zemstvo, with the help of all its district branches, founded a museum, and for this first step wisely selected a house right in the market place, where every man and woman coming to sell hay or eggs or butter, could walk in and see. Soon a great collection of cottage-made furniture, utensils, toys, bowls, fancy boxes, wheels and agricultural implements (as there is plenty of timber round about), fur coats, felt boots and shoes, linens of all sorts and lace, was displayed in the new museum. This was followed by specimens brought from other parts of Russia, with a different technique; even foreign specimens found their way to this peasant museum, some 1,000 miles from Petrograd and some 500 miles from the nearest railway station at the time. A workshop was then added, and improved looms, with an instructor always ready to explain and demonstrate, attracted every market day eager crowds of women. More workshops for other crafts were soon added, not only in the city but in a good many villages, with evening classes for general instruction. Several lace schools were founded and maintained by the district Zemstvos. (The Zemstvo levies taxes on land to cover expenses of public education, roads, hospitals, and every other institution for the weal of its territory. The peasants, being 90 per cent of the population and living on the land, are the main taxpayers.) But this movement could not go very much further without touching the mainspring of the cottage industries. Indeed, what was the use of improving the technique of anything, if the goods were destined for the hands of the sweater, who would not pay a farthing more for better made goods? The Zemstvo of Viatka soon saw the necessity of controlling the market also. It opened a depot in addition to the museum, a regular store, where furniture and other hand-made goods could be bought retail, or on wholesale terms. It also had a shop at Nijni Novgorod during the fair, and in a few years the turnover exceeded £50,000 (500,000 roubles). This allowed the Zemstvo not only to control the prices for work, but also to supply the workers with materials (such as thread, iron fittings, varnishes, etc.) at factory prices.

This put the necessary check on the former despots, the sweaters. They groaned, were furious with the Zemstvos, but had to submit to a real power. Again I will say that all is not ideal; many things could, and should be more artistic, many mistakes are made through lack of properly trained leaders, but as we have no colleges for training leaders and managers of handicrafts worth speaking of anywhere in the world, we have to appreciate even these efforts and learn the offered lesson.

Thousands of instances could be described, but even these few will be sufficient for discussing the question - how to help the workers.

Some day we can enter into details and take one industry after another and discuss the various requirements and means. Today I will try to show a little of the general trend of help as it is given.

In Russia it is usually considered that help must consist in teaching the technique of various sorts of work. In a centre of a certain industry a school is opened, a cheap teacher from Petrograd is sent for, and children are made to learn lace-making or weaving. The teacher, as a rule, is a young girl who went through three years of industrial education at the Imperial School of lace; before this she has learnt to read and write - nothing else. She is often very undeveloped and dull, without any ideas of how to teach. Sometimes an elderly foreign lady milliner or old incapacitated governess, having some friends among the officials, gets this post of instructor, but as the pay ranges between £20 to £25 a year, there are few applicants of this kind.

The teacher teaches what she herself has been taught. The school, with its ready-made principles, is brought from the town into a new world of peasantry, whose life, history, traditions are quite different and perfectly unknown to the town civilisation. The school brings the western methods, the peasantry lives by the eastern traditions. The teaching applies to the surface, the old traditions are concerned with the essence of things.

No attention is paid to what crafts were practiced before the introduction of the school, nor what the methods and traditions were. No one ever thought of this. The grandmothers or even mothers may have possessed a craft with a past of a thousand years, may have possessed methods so elaborate and symbolical that none of these teachers ever could attempt to copy them. I can refer those who like to know more about such methods to the beautiful eight volumes with several thousands of illustrations of the Mordva ornament and needlework by Dr. Haekel, Helsingfors (Price 25 roubles). If the children were left in their mothers' hands they would become as skilled themselves, inhale as it were the fragrance of the work from childhood, sharing its different stages with their mothers. Knowing all this, knowing also this great value of inherited traditions, skill, taste, and symbolism, it is quite painful to see the results of school education. At present all new 'science' (whether it applies to lace or embroidery, weaving or metal work) is chance work. Some 'fashionable' piece of machine lace, perhaps out-of-date in Paris at the time, some metal brooch of a peculiar style, Art nouveau, made by the million in a factory to shine a week or two in high life, which descends gradually to the lower classes, and is sold then in the street for a penny; some 'interesting' effect of machine weaving - a fad of today, the object of disgust tomorrow - all these may take the fancy eye of the undeveloped so-called 'leaders and teachers' and serve as a model for laborious handwork. It then goes through these schools, and is engraved for ever in the young minds of the peasant pupils, as something new and desirable. My memory keeps a multitude of facts, a multitude of efforts, rising and falling, histories of births and deaths of industries - alas, also histories of their crippled childhood, of their faulty, sickly growth. It all looks to an outsider a chaos. Not so to me. One red thread runs through all; its name is separateness.

The workers, the leaders, the producers and the consumers do not love each other, do not know each other. They are groping in the dark, not knowing that they are limbs of one common body, under one common law, that they cannot do without each other. Instead of planned harmony, they work in a chaotic, disorderly, disjointed way. What result can there be but degradation and misery?

In all countries, the handicrafts are going on in various ways, under various influences, driven often to degradation and death by ignorance or greed. Both workers and leaders, middlemen and consumers, are unaware of the colossal magnitude of this universal fact. They take it as purely local, or do not trouble their heads at all, save about cheapness.

One 'leads' in a far away village, perhaps collecting and distributing work to order of some firm in town; another, perhaps a very well meaning soul, living all the year round in the country and having leisure time, and pressed by a famine year, gives small orders to peasants in a philanthropical spirit. Some friends in the same spirit buy and try to spread the goods. Perhaps a high official - friend of the initiator - may procure a yearly stipend; and lo! a new industry is afloat. It may end in a disaster, when there is no knowledge; the goods may not be marketable; or it may prove a success, especially when the initiator learns more than he teaches, brings out the best traditional quality of the workers, all the characteristic strong features; then such goods find their way abroad and get good prices. There may be larger efforts too. One Zemstvo opens a store of peasant industries in Moscow, another in Riazan or Viatka; there are some friendly societies or shareholding companies dealing with peasants' industries, also private shops and a great many local centres of industries scattered all over Russia. There are people eager to lead, to teach, to act as middlemen, some very honest and well-wishing, others greedy and ignorant, large and small sweaters, and there are immensely more workers who are in need of organizations. It is not a thing we can take or leave. It is there: unavoidable, chaotic, and calling for help.

All these channels of organization and distribution of peasant work act separately. Their experiences are not shared or utilized, they do not know each other, they do not realize the common great aim, the common great source; they do not feel the support of a co-worker, co-thinker, co-lover. They repeat the same lessons, make the same mistakes. The valuable experience of one is lost to the thousands of others. In Russia, this separateness is inflicted by the general trend of politics. The rulers find it undesirable to allow the union of various workers, as they know only too well that Union is Strength, and Strength is Power.

If such is the result of separateness in one and the same country, how much more must it reflect on international separateness - how much less do we know, each in our own country, of foreign tastes, and requirements, of foreign markets! Yet the Twentieth Century in its lines of life has in every way gone away from the Nineteenth Century. The world gets smaller and smaller. In olden times we thought of the limits of our village, and then of our province. Now we must study the life and ways of foreign countries, we begin to feel our international message, we begin to join our voice to the symphony of the world.

A Russian provincial may be indifferent to the characteristics and symbols of his own locality, but, bring into his small town Japanese or Hindu goods, or French or Spanish, and see what a commotion it will create. An English lady may get tired of many once tempting things of English-make displayed in Regent Street, yet may be strongly attracted by the original Russian hand made goods, novel to her eye and mind. It is quite natural that we should accommodate ourselves to those new lines. The thinker knows that this intercourse has a far deeper significance than it seems to have from the outside. The ways to the common aim get more and more interlaced, those who tread them become more and more brothers, more and more mutually needed.

The International Union of Arts and Crafts may try to lay the first lines of communion between the various countries. It may join and transcend the old worldwide organisations, add a new note, a new service to them, and draw strength and power through each of their branches, may, as it were, act in every corner of the world by friendly hands.

Central headquarters may be organized in London. This centre may attract to itself handicrafts from all parts of the world, reveal new fields to the seekers of beauty and originality, to the common hunter of novel goods, to the student of ethnography and antiquity, to the mere woman of the world or housewife. From these an exchange of goods may radiate throughout the world, bringing Hindu, English or Japanese work to Russia, Russian and Hungarian to India, and so forth.

To the leaders of industries, to the craftsmen, it will be a source of inspiration and study. To the workers supplying the hand made goods, it will be an outlet and a market which will deal with them not only honestly but intelligently. The machine-goods have established such centres of information and distribution a long time ago. Money is well taken care of. It is only the world's handicrafts, whatever their magnitude, that are neglected, uncared for, because they run in separate efforts. Today the idea of work in unity with love seems yet Utopian, too much in the sky; but so was any other progressive idea on the eve of its realisation in the concrete world. But if mankind is to progress, to evolve, these lines of unity are bound to evolve also, and then it will take proportions undreamt of today.

Large depots of exchange of industries will grow like mushrooms in every large town of every nation; the honest, loving service to workers and consumers is bound to tell on their popularity. The neglected industries will take up strength again; those who live on small plots of land, now unable to support a family all the year round, will then be secure during the winter months, and the towns will be freed from their overcrowded conditions, thus solving one of the greatest problems of the present age.

CPSIA information can be obtained
at www.ICGtesting.com
Printed in the USA
BVHW031408280819
557039BV00006B/763/P